UNDOING HOURS

UNDOING HOURS

SELINA BOAN

NIGHTWOOD EDITIONS

2021

Nightwood Editions
P.O. Box 1779
Gibsons, BC V0N 1V0
Canada
www.nightwoodeditions.com

COVER DESIGN: Angela Yen
TYPOGRAPHY: Carleton Wilson

Nightwood Editions acknowledges the support of the Canada Council for the Arts, the
Government of Canada, and the Province of British Columbia through the BC Arts Council.

This book has been produced on 100% post-consumer recycled, ancient-forest-free paper,
processed chlorine-free and printed with vegetable-based dyes.

Printed and bound in Canada.

LIBRARY AND ARCHIVES CANADA CATALOGUING IN PUBLICATION

Title: Undoing hours / Selina Boan.
Names: Boan, Selina, author.
Description: Poems.
Identifiers: Canadiana (print) 20210106107 | Canadiana (ebook) 20210106158 |
ISBN 9780889713963 (softcover) | ISBN 9780889713970 (HTML)
Classification: LCC PS8603.O226 U53 2021 | DDC C811/.6—dc23

contents

If I'm transformed by language, I am often crouched in footnote or blazing in title. Where in the body do I begin;
—Layli Long Soldier

the plot so far

ask / what is the history / of a word / a lake of commas /
a pause in the muscle of night / a dry river and the snow it
holds / i am afraid of getting this life / wrong / a thick-
rimmed fence / coins settled in a drawer for food / eat half
a lemon and you'll feel fine / i promise

in the dictionary / the nêhiyawêwin word
mahtakoskacikew / translates to / s/he settles or lays
on top of everything / i'll tell you a story / i stained my
hands as a kid in the backyard where i grew / peeling open
walnut shells / trying to find the part i could eat

at sixteen / i scaled the green water tower / settled at the
top for a better view / dreamt mother wasn't young /
driving a vw van cushioned with gas / hands on the wheel
/ wearing fire / *she was* / and i wanted to believe

from the ground up / growing / i never learned the
hul'q'umi'num' name for the place i lived till i was gone /
there are earned stories / names you don't share / i once
slipped into the bay / cracked my feet on dock barnacles
and bled / i wanted so many ways / to settle / our hearts
/ a window / a plot / a piece of land we wanted to call our
own but was / not ours to name

meet cree: a practical guide to language

tires on concrete   motorcycle thrum   pitch
smack of shoe after shoe after shoe
a podcast plays through a wall & a girl sits in a room with a window

she wants to learn her language but can't find the noise   wonders
awe'na na'ha   a girl bristled with sun   fearless as shadows
she wants to find kiya   wants to read herself past syntax
she is noun inflection   light looking   footsteps inside
a word   coming closer

she's a tongue turned over her desk   a muscled red flop   half/
nerved   not/knowing   stumble stutter spill
a difference between want & (l)earn
how the tongue scrapes itself into sound   the girl gathers
what she does not know   into noise

clip of a rez car revving   lake laps & berry coke fizz   bingo
pings   hill humming   her roommate's podcast fades out
in a city near the ocean   she sits in her bedroom
looks up the word for lonely   kakaskeyihtamihk
eyes on the swing of traffic outside   ears like tunnels where sound
    begins to wave

morning in our apartment, a small, wet funeral

i drown a rat in the kitchen sink
tie back my hair and whisper   *sorry.*

cassie on the plastic stool repeats
the rat's good life, hands on her knees

like we share the same body,
hands that pinch and squirm.

cassie on the plastic stool
is a lemon wedge,

soured and nervous,
she repeats the rat's good life.

i tell her, when i was a girl, i was given
the tail of a baby squirrel by my dad.

first animal he ever shot,
placed in a blue box under my bed.

for years, i slept over his story of a BB gun,
a branch and his own dad barking to shoot.

for years, my roommates and i
have been trying to catch the rat party

that surrounds our lives, the after-sound
of heartbreaks and boiling water

through the drain of the tub.
you can hear their teeth at night,

a loud shadow we brush our mouths
to. we spit and bleed and polish.

cassie and i eat breakfast
standing up. try to bleach

the death out of our walls, the brass vents.
we chew cereal and our disbelief

like muscle on a plate,
the rat is an exhausted blade,

a kneecap dislocating
from soft tissue.

this morning, a light
reflective road

disappearing behind us.
i want to carry the rat all day

in the yellow no-frills funeral
shopping bag

i want to take her to the grocery store
and to the library to pick up a book,

suddenly certain she can read,
the weight of her body swinging

so close to mine.

ongoing conversations with my acne

u are like a once-known animal in the sky
of my face, a pattern of bloated stars

running the territory of my cheeks
in wolf form, teeth that pop

snarl and grow only
to eat away the day near mirrors

u feel so grand
i could cry

a blueprint of oil
on the bus ride home from work at night

i can barely see the planets burning above us
bending through the window

in the thesaurus, constellation comes up with luck
future and circumstance

my circumstance is mom
driving her car into a culvert, seeing

photos afterwards—flash bright on the underbelly of the engine
parts unmoving and foggy at night

how u change
is well documented in a selfie album

images of us
angled toward light like fireweed

the future is my cousin
in a dream where bugs leak from her body

teal beetles that reflect
the syllabus of earth, rearranged

the luck isn't always easy to find
like my attempts to be funny

in a poem

auntie dries her hair in the bathroom
kohkom's slippers shuffle across beige carpet

dreams i keep having
u float off my face like raspberry-red bubbles

remind me where we come from
part prairie, part invasion

u are me made uneven
pushing ur way into this world during sleep

i don't always understand dreams tho
even when i know i should listen

u heal over time   into a lake
into a latch of memory

a run, a burn, a beck

> our bodies are our libraries—fully referenced in memory,
> an endless resource, a giant database of stories.
> —Monique Mojica

your name   a story
of moss tiptoeing its way along the
underbelly of language, river eyes like the
crack of fat when a hide is peeled away,
taste of elk, raw and soft in your teeth at
easter dinner, pop of blood running on
your plate, this is the half story of a boy,
a man, a father who was tripped, round-
lipped stumble a stream (a run, a burn, a
beck), the ground and the getting up again,
nuns marching across a field in the snow
with their forgiveness and their stew, a
girl, a woman, a mother who was making,
this is you, daughter, all your quiet wants
and none of your knowing, a feeling that
wants to stick to the skin but can't quite
remember how, rock, paper, river, you girl
are a gamble made during the planting of
trees, a pickup truck and a bump of plastic
beads stitched by hand, a clot of years
you don't know how to carry and the
fear that this body is not   where
you belong

in six, the seasons

summer

between the warmth of language
and a four-walled room, a girl clicks beginner
cree on the internet, a divided circle,
a laptop, a desk and a full screen
of a flat skyline hung below
the word

> nîpin
> summer in northern saskatchewan
> thick with mosquitoes
> july hatching
> heat

learning the seasons into six
a girl listens to her father's first language
alone, never having been that far north
she hears a sound like a knee-pin
a forced fracture, fixed
with alloy and rods

fall

a girl grows up only to trip again
falls into her not-knowing like a knife
dreams every season, a birth
father's voice   in nêhiyawêwin
she'll imagine

            takwâkin
            how leaves commit themselves
            to change
            how grass rolls gold
            moose velvet lost to the land

she practises aloud, looks up to see
her neighbours dart   between rooms
words bristle   like the city at night
live under concrete, a breath of letters
take-away-a-kin is not the right way
to hear it, her tongue tries   and falls

freeze-up

site to site her fingers touch glass
lake sheen zoom, a picture,
a freezing rain warning for the prairies
white letters against a red screen
on google, she searches
omosôma's seasons into sound

        mikiskâw
        for when language braids
        the ground still again
        and the ice moves in
        cracks closing

a girl can search the space between
a season and a scow, a boat unbound
where words float rivers
swim the surface, here
here, here

winter

a girl in a room in the wrong month
can repeat one season 296 times or more,
an elder's voice stretched
from the laptop screen, power speaks

        pipon
        water solid
        and a thumb of trees
        exposed

her lung sound
a vowel pulled into the snow
a sound it out write it down
try try again,
long reasons to keep repeating

spring

a bulb of light, a breath,
door open like a square of sun
the girl taps in to a woman's voice
she's never heard before, a wish
the web an elder's word

       sîkwan
       sound combed into lake water
       goose necks
       settled into the shape of questions

she hears a sequin of mother's english
disc-shaped bead
balanced
and weighed on the tongue

breakup

a girl between two dialects
still a screen and still a searching, learns
the season of breakup
another word for spring
can come before or after
depending on where you grew up
online, back and forth
a word in the mouth tumbles

>   miyoskamin
>   birch-sapped june
>   season snow spotted
>   river melt
>   running

child again
wrists and creek bone
a river-girl
slick with mud
frost and word-melt
this poem takes place in her imagination
this poem takes place

miyoskamin me and you are s-kin
miyoskamin me and you are s-kin
miyoskamin

in ohkoma's language
where verbs never stand alone
a girl's tongue curls nêhiyawêwin
into the nerves and walks from a room
to where miyoskamin returns
and ice   opens

how to find your father

1. peel his name like an orange. like the skin on your hands. peel
   hours apart. sit so long in that cafe your tea gets cold. pick at
   your thumb till there's blood.

2. when the landlady's dog barks, shrug your coat to the floor. roll
   your head across the computer keyboard. stretch your arms to
   form a muscled y in the air before beginning your message.

3. odds are, if you use his name, cousins will emerge from the
   grass, from beaded felt, from twitter, they will appear like nîpîy,
   spilling into the shape of angled mirrors.

4. as a kid, learn quick that being *native* is *okay* as long as you aren't
   too native, as long as your skin is as yt as it is, as long as you're
   pretty, and you fit in with the other yt kids, and you don't talk
   too much, don't make ppl uncomfortable, read fantasy books at
   lunch against the portable.

5. google the definition of *find*. as a verb, it is to meet, to perceive
   by chance or with effort. as a noun, the act of "discovery,"
   typically of archaeological *interest*. laugh at this. google your
   own face. google his name, over and over again until he appears
   in a profile photo, holding a fish.

6. begin with hello. begin gently, without anger or expectation.
   begin with what you think you know.

7. the day after one of your cousins gets married, there will be
strings of lights coiled along the railing of the porch. eat leftover
food, heated in the microwave. in the kitchen, scrape silver
skin into the compost with your mother. anger will sear what
you cannot yet touch. when you growl with shame, it will claw
inside your stomach.

8. repeat his name. where he was last seen. all your aunties and
uncles. all your cousins. sibling. nieces and nephew. his name.

9. the hardest part. get yourself onto a bus. pull calm from your
jacket. when he walks out of the elevator, be prepared for the
way time will speed up like eyes following earth through a car
window. peel awkward laughter back. watch it blister and gush
onto the sidewalk. let it carry you both.

love poem on a break

Perhaps the hardest thing about losing a lover is
to watch the year repeat its days.
—Anne Carson

His leaving is black spruce swallowed down to the lung. A thumbprint
of where I thought we would be. To begin and to end
always feels like an impossibility. Like a boy trying to see
the eclipse through a Mountain Dew wrapper. Like fibres
sprouting from the body, string-like, in a disease doctors
refuse to believe is real. It's Saturday, or maybe it's Wednesday.
Either way, we begin the work of undoing ourselves in its middle.

His sublet bed stripped down to the hard shine of a blue mattress.
My quiet is a shake of pine and his hands don't recognize
this ending; folding shirts back into themselves,
folding his hands into mine. My want is a stack of endless hours
with him. The red-orange of a river filled with veins; heart unstoppable
    and floating.

Does he remember how nervous I was, asking him on that first walk?
How he leaned his body sweet, not yet touching.
Grass up to my waist. His arm near my arm. Prickle and fizz.
He taught me tenderness can live in the body after all.
Him on a dock kissing my forehead. Him juggling lemons in the grocery store.
A joke about how much of our lives we spend in lines, waiting.

That summer and next, I became convinced Ottawa had given me fever.
Humid stickiness unlike home. For three days, he called in sick with me.
We hid from sun, shared ice cubes, froze our bodies as best we could.

A losing is a leaving is a kiss. Sometimes it's true, we laugh
and cry at the same time. We believe *everything is going to be ok.*
We sit face to face, legs over legs, and hold on.
Our names in each other's mouths—torched clocks.

my mother's oracle cards said

the answer is simple. take your mess,
bless it and start over.

bacon fat in a tin, i spend mornings alone
eating the dead in strips. sleeveless
girl with the eyes of my kohkom,
i leak the moon. hair greasy from sleep,
placing sticky notes onto the objects
i am learning to name.

sâsâpiskisikan   frying pan
tahkascikan   fridge
wâsênikan   window

summer this year is me smacking
my mouth up against lessons.
the bite and roll and cry of it.

shot of black each morning—
a three-legged dog on my mother's porch,
ears like sharpened moons, turning.

does fire have a sound before it happens?

this afternoon, i cried over a locked jar.
a wet towel bundled under the sink.
i cried over nothing and everything,
breasts swollen with the month.

time a circle, in parallel, all at once,
my mother's radio singing for water.

there are 840 fires, count undone.
a thousand possible lakes underneath
this kitchen, raging.

ask ourselves, how did we get here?

i'll keep sticking notes to the wâsênikan till i learn,
body bleeding kisses for no one but the ground
and my grandmothers.

body humour

mom stands on a kitchen chair / stretches her hand out toward the fire
alarm / to silence the screaming

we laugh at screaming things / we cut off our heads / we body humour

hair tied back / mom stops walking in the middle of a story / she
re-enacts how granddad slipped at the gas station / how miraculously
close he came again to cracking his skull / caught him an inch to
concrete / in the flex of her elbow like a hockey headlock

i love her in the same way it hurts to lose you / like the tree inside my
body keeping me upright has burned / orange flickering mass / all ash /
scooped next to jars of popcorn kernels / fields of beads and zippers

at age three / i told her i was a bad guy / with a gun / a knife / and a
fork / she transcribed the memory of me looking tough into a piece
of art / my bad-guy declaration next to a photo of me / wearing a
multicoloured bucket hat and a face so fierce i keep trying to conjure it

what i'm trying to say is / i've spent the last few years ferrying my sad /
uncertain life over water every few months / to visit her / to stand with
my back to the fire / as she suggests how best to fill the after-space of
regret / observing the way it holes through my life in all directions

we crack up cleaning the kitchen at midnight / recount dating stories /
nice is just another word for boring / she says / her hand swiping crumbs
into a cloth / *no one wants to be nice*

when we moved she wrote *good clothes* in black sharpie on a
cardboard box / good thing for the briefest of moments / the
tenderness of watching her place her lunch in a glass jar / waking to my
nickname / on an envelope

love in motion unfolds / hovering over the shine of ground / the way
sadness sometimes does / making you belly laugh / glimmering / like a
dilated eye close to fire / it waves you over / collects sticks after a storm
/ places them in a green bucket to burn

small talk

Outside our meeting spot, the city is a drive-through of wet foil.
Windows and traffic lights reflect through the rain and come back
blurry. You ask if I'm hungry and my yes wraps itself around the night,
offering purpose. The coils of my stomach lurch and I am all bubbles,
chatting the way I do with people I don't know very well.

Anything fried. Salty. I used to eat dirt as a kid when I could.

We are strangers with the same cheeks, smiling numbly. We walk the
borderlands of our faces together, blink at sale signs in bright pinks and
greens, everything 50 percent off. You say because we're Cree we should
be good with directions and we laugh at that, circling the same blocks
again and again, searching for somewhere to eat. Two bodies on Google
Maps, making a small blue dot at the crosswalk.

This way? We've passed this before. Clouds. Rain today. Most days, yeah.

You joke about time and I rebuild a world with our shoulder blades,
infinite years already soaked and tanned into our history. Tell the
sidewalk a joke and it will crack up with earth, dandelions petalled
yellow like the T-shirt I got from a moving sale last summer.

This summer. Road trip. Visits. As long as you like.

Everything is closed so we circle back to Timmy's on the corner. We
stand in line and our chatter becomes grey carpet collecting rainwater,
holding the runoff of shiny questions.

Just tea. A muffin. I already ate. Water please.

Small talk as window, as a lack, as too much, as nerves, a bucket of my baby teeth rattling under the table. All nerves and forgiveness. All, how bright this moon, who is who and how are they, and what are they like? We sit in plastic chairs beside the maroon-coloured half wall, separating the place you wait and the place you sit to face each other.

I had a feeling. I had a dream. I dreamt of you.

Small talk as invention. As something we place between us to feel more comfortable. On the way back, you stop at the 7-Eleven. I wait beside the ATM and look at the rows of packaged chips and sweet tarts. You are a lake of jokes. The machine flutters and you press money into my palm. Insist. Absolution. You say cab and I shake my head. Alone on the ride home,

Salt. Where again. Rain. Who again.

in cree there is no word for half/brother

had i grown up with you, maybe we would've learned
to talk first in gesture, watch words form
from the end of our hands like bubbles
babbling wave after wave of kid-speak.

                                    today, in my ~~vancouver~~ apartment
                        where tub water runs orange & silverfish slip
                                    through book glue & tile cracks,
                            i learn the cree word for older brother
                                    & wonder how to say it out loud.
                                nistes, i still can't say for sure

how we were kids, red
halved by waniyihcikewin.
my best guess is you know
the hook of survival,
how to laugh when a room needs it.
you can sink the eight ball in pool with side spin,
know kohtâwinaw's stories like revolving coins.

                                    in the past beside this one,
            you tease me   because i don't like eggs without ketchup
                            because when you're out late, i worry
            you still remember the toque i stole from you in grade eleven,
                            the one you'd pulled down close to your eyes.

i know now that ohi in cree
looks like, oh, hi, but means
relative; or these ones here;
these things, here,

> where kohtâwinaw worked at a bed & breakfast
> up north   the place i first meet you
> my hands shaky a gesture toward your name
> a way to say hello.

inside this hour / another hour inside / another hour

in the field of hours that hangs between us,
a mint-scented tree swings on the rear-
view mirror. you tap the beat to an eighties
country song like APTN dads do

slouch of music   on the road again. *lord, i
hope this day is good* on repeat. we drive past
a river, your elbow out the window, going so
fast, i had to google the lyrics for this poem

you translate memory for me inside a bundle
of jokes inside a spiral of locks inside this
truck inside these hours. i carve *lol* on a gas
station styrofoam cup with my fingernails,
trace over the indented letters with a pencil.
something i learned as a kid. roll the cup on
paper, see what appears again / what words
carry

you were hired once by big oil to sit in the
room and be the NDN ok with it all. *didn't feel
right,* you said. we chew gum, drive highways
like years, our lives side by side, all this time

i am slow hours / resurfacing / can't stop
laughing green. out of my mouth grows
wild rye, arching toward the ground. i see a
wrinkled poem inside the truck's plastic cup
holder. i learn how kiyâm feels in the body,
a shrug of the shoulders / a deep orange sky
inside you

most days / i rot

/ outside sears, you tell me in the truck how
like my brother you are, counting everything.
you wear the skins of kisewâtisiwin, stretch
a kindness over what has been hard. stolen /
selves / branching at our feet

there is a stack of apologies / hung on the
door / of this hour / swinging an endless
loop of getting / honest / with ourselves /
your could-be daughter saying pimâtisiwin /
paskeyâw / time / it branches off in

another direction / it leans out the window
of a truck and nods   *see you soon, my girl*

minimal pairs are words holding hands

kisik (and also)

kisik, she texts, *it's refreshing*, dating a girl who doesn't want to talk every day.

it's been two months since i walked on concrete in platform shoes and my heart still hurts.

kísik (the sky)

sometimes love unschools me. it is the smell of juniper, how bracelets sound against each other, a river filling with water.

it is a blue mirror and the way the world listens via kísik.

pisiw (a lynx)

i watch my roommate move the soil of one plant to another in the sink.
she tells me her dreams while opening cupboards. a pisiw in the alley on her way to a party, hair burning.

pêsiw (bring someone)

pêsiw who speaks their mind at your ex's wedding, shines jokes under the table like a flashlight.
humour is a beacon. you can't catch laughter from someone you don't know, or don't like.

niya (me/i)

this summer is a planet and the yous in this poem are exes, missing family, general advice, niya.
this summer is a house party. overhearing someone say, that *native girl*, she was so *well-spoken*.

niyâ (lead/go ahead)

you niyâ me to the place they found his body. your own body, a lit window, a quiet x-ray.
words vibrate worlds if you listen.

niyanân (us)

i took a photo of the window, the snow. none of nohtâwiy. i hold niyanân in my mind. his face in mine. days fit into the holes where my wisdom teeth once were. blood, nerve.

niyânan (five)

if-i-dream-polysynthetic-if-i-dream-nêhiyawêwin-will-i-finally-speak-will-nohkom-hear-me? i missed knowing her in this world by niyânan years so it's my friends who teach me to stop remaking all my bead lines.

sakahikan (a nail, for building)

in grade six, i snuck a tin of blue eyeshadow to school. fingers blue from touching myself.
in my apartment, sakahikana push back out of the floor, rip holes where we walk.

sâkahikan (a lake)

my mother's microwave doesn't have time, just two neon dots stacked and blinking.
so much dust on her bathroom blinds it forms a sâkahikan. a horizontal universe of skin cells. pollen, hair.

44

kóna (snow)

outside esso, kóna starts rounding itself up in my ears. the world gone sideways.
when anxiety stretches up into your body, look around and ask yourself, are you safe?

póna (put it in the fire)

you slept in a sleeping bag, rolled your jacket into its own hood and prayed it wouldn't rain.
tonight, póna. star guts and the space between your fingers where night appears.

ôma (this)

today, my heart is a staircase. i am incapable of the love others deserve.

ôma is my apology. a gas station on the way to visit nohtâwiy. the room you and i once shared.

ôta (here)

isn't it funny how we can remember at the same time we forget?

ôta, where we first hold hands, become the mouths words camp inside, for a while, at least.

what you miss doesn't always matter and vice versa

fathers as road trips / as borrowed cars / a thousand likelihoods /
smoking at the sink / washing plates / to billie holiday / swaying / *love
is funny or it's sad / it's quiet or it's mad* / i am matter / and un-matter /
mad / and not mad / chrome nails that change colour / under angles
of sun /

i learn / from the people we love / laughter is contagious /   here /
take / this laughter / this ordinary day / where a lake is a belly button
/ where the day is a joke you told once in the car in cree / about a
man and a fart / or a hill / or something involving wind / passing / a
moment of relief / grass all over this highway /

                         me and fathers / exist / in a thousand prairies /
like matter / in different / phases / your water glass beside your bed /
an air freshener in the glovebox / how close you've been to lightning in
the bush / learning to / take up space / kid me meets dad you / grown
me / meets kid you / dad you meets / grown me / you were looking
in / a mirror / you were / bottling apology / writing my name / in a
facebook message /   we love who we love / faces puffy from /
trying / we exit this hour / en route / to a different day / and

ongoing conversations with nitôn

> We knew that our language came before the world.
> —Terese Marie Mailhot

this forest has the lip ring of ur teenage dreams
spun moss so metal it hurts

u grind ur teeth hard
battle urself like pikachu versus pikachu

electric shock that burns everyone
except the grass

inside u
language is a mosh pit

it spits shoves grins
sweats rivers, pulls hailstorms

it is push of aster, lake grunt
in memory before memory

u learn, nepiwahcâw
the ground is wet

like the middle of u
all ur failures line up as teeth

familiar and necessary
like leaving ur body for a time

u believe u are not enough if ur not loved
watch a woman u just met undress at the lake

unbutton jean shorts, slip morning off
near empty slurpee cups, leftover

brain freeze, u swallow
indecent in ur missing of other lips

the intimacy of kissing
language, a lightning strike

between selves
rare and unforgiving

like the taste of armpit sweat

water, u drink
to live

ur grief holding
like a day, inside

prayer for endless sky
u know

tumble and fling
language like a lighter

like a flame turning   to dance

alter, ego

after Monica McClure

serena   doesn't care if u like her
in the kitchen, shoulder to shoulder
she is a zipper   teeth pulled open to peer inside
the party's tongue   quipping with u in the hallway

serena   scrubs her teeth in the bathroom
with someone else's toothbrush
spits orange dorito dust into a sunset
an earwig softening under her shoe

serena   is the right kind of mean
pressing memory's button
she'll tease u till u like her
she'll make fun of ur band tee
start a fight if u fuck with her friends
isn't always just kind mean

serena   is hot glue pressing herself to the party's seam
is inside a sex dream about maggie gyllenhaal
is sliding marshmallows onto her fingers
is hot fries

serena   watches molly blow pubic hair off the toilet like dandelion seeds
she pees a toilet-bowl monologue
marinates her lungs in smoke   watches bathroom tiles turn teal
like a music video, swallowing a crowd of scratchy towels

serena   is relaxed sway   holding her own hand
is u too   but not
is forgetting is   so much more well-liked   is   ignition
coils   is sporadic txts
is coming

with love,

—for all my roommates

we roommate and switch   door propped open by a woven
handbag   door propped open by a mirror   by reservoir water
cutting itself   through our names

we   dandelion ideas of home blow on the edges

worry-chatter on the porch   we flip our bodies on all sides in sun
we roommate and forget ourselves for a while

a man arrested near our windows one summer   so close we heard his
feet outside on grass so close

we build bikes   shake winter through our hair   a snowball fight that
runs through the back door of time   rattling laughter

we roommate   and grief *which is never not missing someone, it is living
and missing at the same time*

we open and close

try to sing ourselves to sleep three days in a row   can't rest   crunch
chip bags together as night ritual instead

we twenty and age   curl fear up   curl up against cellphone
light   swipe ourselves into morning

we roommate and fall in love, too

in the dark one night   the most tender first kiss   shy and hissing

some nights, time stretches itself under door light from our closed bedrooms,
headphones as collective quiet

we unstick and pull, we chain-smoke hours

we place mixing bowls under the sink to catch leaks, peer
underneath   make

sure the water holds

emails with nohtâwiy

i lift you from an email and into a dream.
    i hang a blue hip bone my cousin painted
    on my bedroom wall.
    when i undo time, it is a thousand lichens attached
    to a branch. a crowd of emails, singing aloud, swaying to the
    words.

see you soon?

you pray
    and i make a church with my hands.
    here is the pinkied steeple, built next to wiggling nails.
    here are all the people i have not yet met
        who pray or don't pray
        who offer me crackers and cheese later in this story
        who orbit your life and are family, too.

i'm owed nothing
    the brief hinge of time won't heal
    between us   there is static
    inside this daughter email i send to you
    offered days late, an after to your updates
        my nieces are learning constellations
        NDN fb memes
        kohkom's leather work.

i lift you from a dream into an email.
a dog squeals like a tire outside.
you as magnet, as turbine, rotating back into my life.
i write myself mundane and friendly.
this morning when i kiss time
it's the sun's reflection off a car window.
it's my future kids, with dirt in their hands,
chattering to you about yarrow and telling fart jokes.

see you soon?

easy enough to say a prayer.
to hold your own hands and look up.
i'm not religious but i have prayed.
i want to ask, how does your faith guide decisions?
do you choose the prairie or the sea?
do you move for someone you love?
does it make it easier?
at dinner, i watch you say grace when my eyes
should be closed. i write the moment into a poem
and send it to you.

campaign for my body's mess

tonight, mcdonald's
is my saviour   i drink
water   like i'm in gridlock
burning in the sun without a/c
an accident slowing everyone
on the highway   radios turned
on to flashes of grief
memory   blasts itself
through me   a pillow
in a window display
that says *leave*
your shit somewhere
else   it crowds the river
near where mom set fire
to sap as a girl
dime-sized leaks
from the tree just enough
to make light run
toward the ground
i   drink till   memory
stops forming nohtâwiy
stops messaging   prays
every night to jesus
in gratitude
too easy some days
becoming the things
i fear   i'm too soft
for the internet
have the urge to put

my head on the shoulders
of bus strangers   daddy
issues a collection of key chains
i've been accumulating
rabbit-fur puffs
beaded strawberries
on a metal ring   i wear
headphones to watch porn
sound maxed   i pick my nose
in elevators scratch
time off the walls
in the form of glossed
paint   faux wood
inside this grief
forest   guts are a deer
hung sliced
in my grandpa's shed
a pool of blood on the concrete
of this day   i find
a piece of grass
maskosiy   inside the x-ray
of nisit like a fleck
of green glitter   shining
i press a button
and a hamburger
appears

2.1.a questions and answers

Q: *kîkwây ôma*   *what is this*

a leak in memory

a love story that doesn't travel all the way to the end

his forehead against a bus window

his hand between his thighs

he stood cutting onions, tucking his fingers in

when nohtâwiy messaged back

he sat on the wooden bleachers with me

overlooking the public pool and that strange baby-blue stage

where a group of parents danced to a bluetooth speaker

he told me particles in the air make for good sunsets

held my loss between his shoulder blades

a leak in memory

a love story that doesn't travel all the way to the end

what are endings   tho

                              but another way to know time

                    to place in the centre of our learning   a hand of minutes

A: maskosiy anima   that is a blade of grass

                                              a sharp stagger across memory

                                                              my first time

                                            at a party hot-boxing a bathroom

                                            socked feet in the centre of the tub

                                                    i am a pack of matches

                                              waiting for the friction of light

                                                      how do our legs look

                                                          dressed in smoke

                                                          do we stay young

                                                            when we leave

                                  we leave outlines of our bodies on the wall

Q: *maskasiy cî awa*   *is this a fingernail*

in the mouth of memory

pulled apart like the insides of a clock

undoing hours

a bundle of wâpanêwask   unfurls

NDN time stretches grassland over a watch and is never late

i scrub my hands

and the pieces of a story wash up on the bank

i lost my lover and nohtâwiy in the same month

pull missing

hair from my head

in the mirror   i watch time drip

into a lake   into a love letter   into a poem

Possible Answers:

namôya, maskosiy anima   *no, that is a blade of grass*

                          at a party hot-boxing a bathroom

namôya, maskasiy ana   *no, that is a fingernail*

                          in the mouth of memory

namôya, maskasiy ana,   *no, that is a fingernail,*

maskosiy anima.   *that is a blade of grass.*

email drafts to nohtâwiy

i call you by your first name.

you and i, like aspen talking to each other underground. messages
threading through roots that run beyond us. the summers we visited
are an elastic stretched between time, holding keys and junk-drawer
magnets together. in this version of events, we aren't just poems.

i'll admit, i've been afraid to write. so here is my deflection, for
everyone to read.

this summer, my roommate nadia got caught in a storm. hair gelled
with so much glitter it beamed across her eyebrows like wet stars. one
night near the apartment, a boy offered me a piggyback ride, told me
my crutches were no good without padding, asked if my hands were
sore, holding his own in the air like fireworks. days weren't always as
long as we imagine now.

you told me being patient is part of being cree and i'm trying. i'm
learning this world is not the only place we visit. that kohkom keeps
visiting your dreams with stories from mine. that the heart doesn't need
a brain or a body to keep beating. and that sounds about right.

i keep looking in the mirror now and seeing you. both of us, capable of
giving ourselves; we believe in love that hard.

your heart is held in beat by a battery. my heart wobbles through a new
breakup. we both steady ourselves for the next thousand years. i want to
make you so many dinners, fold a berry pie from our lands. A butter crust
i've been perfecting for a year now, so you see the layers on each slice.

now here's a story, you said. summer is a rope, connecting the lake to seasons. you sit in traffic and i clean gutters, pull out a dead bird, a rat. pick raspberries, purple juice on my t-shirt. wasp stings. summer is a rope holding us together. an honouring, an anger. forgiveness, a softball magnet on the fridge.

in this poem,   we are sitting at a kitchen table till morning   so early now   we have to squint our eyes   in the light to see

i didn't know the future would be another love poem

after our breakup, highways flatten further and further into my brain
cementing distance   between   ppl i try to date who are not you.

a truck passes with a green bumper sticker, *shift happens*
and it's supposed to be funny   sliced body of a forest in the back.

we move through time   eating sugared coke bottles, watching
kids make salsa and pork chops on TV   thighs touching, your sad eyes
    made my eyes

sad too. in an after-dream, we sit on a picnic table and explain
our lives after time. i stay in bed just to keep talking to you.

in an after-visit, we undress what is left of one another,
a sweater scrunched on my bedside table, the bottom of your backpack

where   late afternoon spills   light
flooding   every *i miss you* back to memory

        what happens when we burn everything good in our lives?

at the airport, winter inhales and swallows me whole
as my everyday buttons itself out of yours.

this after without you is a ghost. you clip basil and place it
on the desk. two bright green leaves folding into each other.
you watch roots grow in water. shield me from the wind at a stop-

light. grief is a circle inside me. a hand shaky with *should-haves*, capable of misting a tropical plant. of baking a pie.

heartbreak feels so small in the world. it is two foreheads touching so close to a kiss it hurts.

on wanting

when i message you, my phone autocorrects the beginning—*hey, I hope*—becomes

—*hope, hope*—and i imagine your brief bubbling ellipsis, like water suspended on the awning of a tent, becomes the reply—*yeah, we could all use more hope, on any given day*

in nêhiyawêwin, the grammar of telling time includes the word mîyâskam to describe something that happens in the first half of an hour. it's how we say after

mitâtaht cipahikanis mîyâskam nîso tipahikan / ten minutes after two o'clock and the day is aluminum / non-magnetic / silvered with touch / i close my blinds / open my bedside drawer / turn my vibrator on

i practise time in my dress / kekâc is almost / kekâc nisto tipahikan / it's almost three o'clock / it's kekâc a bad day / taped up like the hem of my skirt / to hold for the afternoon / till it falls to its original length / below my knees / above my ankles / this day slips through the clock / kekâc tipiskâw / kekâc niyânan tipahikan / time translates / i was a mistake / into lake glimmer / thigh-high socks and fur buttons

last night at the party, molly asks me—*who do you perform for?*—and the question rotates through my whole life, girls swiping girls swiping boys, bobby pins in their hair, *the internet knows i'm single*, i laugh and we smoke, talk crows, exes, car rides that filter into the next day, this day a denim jacket with corduroy lining, sleeves rolled to show the green underneath after is mîyâskam / an orgasm / crotch sweat / a towel slung over the chair / mîyâskam âpihtâtipiskâw / my want is a mood ring / it glows lavender close to the body / mîyâskam âpihtâtipiskâw / i vaseline my lips / i watch a red lily take root in my sternum

when i message you my phone autocorrects the beginning and nostalgia crawls through a window to rearrange the room, curtains opening in or through to someplace else, like the spot where beads hang from an earlobe you want to kiss, a field prickled with goldenrod, the sound of buttons shaking loose

suck it up <3

nausea is a quarry   the bottom
of a lake pulled for gravel

                        pebbles of time   loosened
                        & poured into a body of roads

                                    i dreamt a daughter stunning   with scales
                                    i dreamt wâpanêwask healing toothaches
                                                burn fever

on the bedside table   gravol
that pink pill   a miracle

                        in suppository form
                        another way into ourselves

                                    when i can't sleep
                                    i meditate on my own lungs

bleed myself into other women
a jar of water kept beside the bed

                        for blackouts or thirst   my mood is full of holes
                        like burnt clay, the moon

                                    last night   i went looking for someplace
                                    to hide the river   selfish girl

trying to hold what can't be held
making everything romantic

                              on the dance floor   hair swings
                              sharp & elastic as the truths

                                          we tell ourselves
                                          to make heartbreak hurt less

via email nohtâwiy always signs off
blessings   bless this

                  ever-changing tuesday
                  this city i am learning to un-name

                                      inside the bar   i crowd myself clean again
                                      body a feedback loop

a GIF of spinning neon hearts
a cell no bigger than an apple seed

                                    capable of remaking an animal   each piece
                                    of self a brand-new self

                                      the ceiling keeps screaming at me
                                    who knew

we would be so mortified
by how ordinary our lives are

in a food court stuffed with babies
& angry warm mouths   we visit

our names   daughter   nohtâwiy
surrounded by a ceiling of red lights

mannequins wearing fur-collared t-shirts   a fence of tinsel
we buy family presents   are not offered gift wrap

we look at our phones
click   scroll   light

we live & our decisions   turn into a story
ka nihtâ mihtatamihk

sometimes we pay for the things
we know   soap in the mouth

back at the bar   jess sits
elbows on the table

tilting a glass of water   back   &   forth
she reminds me

love is when you laugh at yourself
& mean it   take what you're given

& give it   i was swept back
& forth over a road in december

                    badly timed
                    road trip in snow

if nohtâwiy could hear me in this poem   i would whisper
i just wanted to be near you   i just

                    wanted to undo this grief on our hands
                    melt the ice in the bucket by the door

                              kiyâm   let it go   for your own self
                              emoji shrugs remind me

doubt can live in the body
like a town shaking itself to sleep

                    i've learned when you buy a knife
                    at the mall   you get one sharpening for free

run the hurt

through water / through grass / along the river where reeds brush
blood skin pus / where pain lets itself out little by little / there are
words you don't want to write / a shape of history denied so many
times   violence forms a country

if you are hurting / if you are uncertain / know that this body / can
hold itself to itself and undo at the same time / it is your grandmother
lying in bed underneath a blue wool blanket / an article she cut from
the newspaper waiting for you beside the sink / it is kohkom saying
kisâkihitin with her hands / stitching beads to a leather purse you will
one day hold / it is your questions to her / on love / sovereignty / just-
washed hair / learning in nêhiyawêwin that verbs are at the centre /
how we move through this world / a heart / blue red yellow / flowers
circling each other / is to feel / shake / kiss / to love so fiercely /   it is
a sky

<∩V°

the way an ice cube melts in the pocket between your teeth and cheek,
i want to soften into my own body, move beyond this hour into the now
of gentle futures, the nows of summers all glitter and hope-scotch
joi's signs in nêhiyawêwin neon LED—ᐱᐧᐨ

what i mean to say is, i meant to make something more of myself today
i can't just say i want to learn the words sâkihitowin and pimâtisi
in nêhiyawêwin   colours are verbs—things are being blue,
are being green—and inside my fridge, last night looks like circles
of creamed fat gone sour, half a lime on a box of eggs

inside my mouth is a flooding apartment, where a fig plant grows a
mushroom at its root, where i circle the floor, mispronouncing words
and laughing with the snap and wave of breath everywhere, cupboards
and salt floating through this world, down moss-soaked stairs

how grammar knows us, how i'm learning to hold it together and undo
myself in the city, to take my tongue off and put it on again, a bright
neon-pink sign—*don't you dare be ashamed,*   *don't you dare be shy*

have you ever fallen in love with a day?

that senselessly beautiful way light filters through a forest—all gold body,
   all quiet sway
so soft on the inside u get drunk on it
pine cones hanging   from ur brain
a shelter from the teeth of animals, morning ice, love's shadow

ur learning ur language on twitter   googling the weather in nêhiyawêwin
tânisi ê-isi wêpahk
how is the weather being flung?
copper wires of rain heaved like a body touching itself
over this day, drowning all undershirts and sorrow

most days u hate urself   play online poker with the currency of skittles
enter anonymous chat rooms to meet other women
u leave band-aids in the river   dye ur roommate's hair
with blue gloves on the back porch   leaves starting to brown
the ends of her in ur hands

if sadness is a legacy so is joy
and so, payipâstêw—the sun shines through a hole in the clouds
and in this forest, moss crawls up ur legs   tinted with heat
curled like eyelashes under metal

how to be as lovable and dangerous as the sun?
how to love like a day?   not endlessly but with care
for every forest or room u touch   every spot there is light

all you can is the best you can

i've decided not to tell
the whole story as i know it

i know, it's not what we gut
& organ against, it's not

how we imagined that gentle
unbolting of something truth-like

from between our rib cages
a phone cord pulling itself

out of the past through a body
of email drafts & facebook messages

unsent   family ghosts hover
could-bes across the spine of a story

nohtâwiy in the backyard
hands pulling light

translucent dandelions
from the ground

hands pulling rats from the walls
pulling prayer into his body

read the passage
so you also must forgive / so you also must

*

forgive me, i don't remember
how we got here exactly, which lie i kept

which truth i made, palm smacking
against the hood of a car

tracing backwards each pothole
in the asphalt of our lives

gaps so wide   in my mind
i bus sixteen hours, two days, one month

to recognize the loop
flattened past road

i visit nohtâwiy by plane & a field
grows across the street, husked green

i step through his home's stuccoed entry
& see two of my nieces, eyes

steady through the stair
balusters, like two jumper cables

fusing me to their dreams
nail-polish stickers, dinosaur spines

hi
echoes like ultrasound

in the future days
we hot lava the floor

a slush of molten cushions
i become a bridge between

the couch & table
hands on my back

my nephew pulls an island
from his sock

& we all leap to safety
breath giddy & sugared

this memory
is the kind night buses drive through

when i can't sleep
i worry they will forget me

pace the battery of my heart
try to talk like family

hear, here, see
daughter-proof noisy   undeniable

kindness a bed, a photo of nohtâwiy
with his arm slung around the head of a bear

at the kitchen table
he recalls words

tawâw, tansi
i'm a flare of sun

blasting through each year
sudden & spitting

i brush my teeth
upstairs

i cry that first night
overwhelmed

by my own stranger
blinking back at me

                    *

nohtâwiy & i
visit the pigs, an afternoon

of pink bellies
turned to the red

heat of the lamp
on our skins

do they have names?
i ask

breathing in
damp straw

over the wooden latch
nohtâwiy leans

to place his hand close
to their mouths

opens to offer them cut apple

it's the kids
who do the naming

he says, rinsing
his palms

with water from a cup
turning

to open the door
in his chest

there's a steel valve
fixed to his heart

pumping time backwards
keeping him alive

a PhD in street smarts, he says
a kitchen joke

time-stamping every tooth
he & i lost

*

i grew up

took myself too seriously
on repeat, i loved vicious

tender & unremarkable
this poem

isn't what i'd hoped
a window into the territory

of love   i take
slices of pie to jess & brandi

lend red
thread to edge earrings

how anger turns
itself

over time, asking if love
is a decision

or not
is it

memory
you don't recognize

but know is true
calcified into prayer

on my knees, i sand
baseboards with my mom

make lunch in the dust

i eat & eat & am greedy
i want & want & am sad

*

what was i supposed to say
to my brother when we met?

an unplanned visit at moores
between stacks of buttoned shirts

plastic torsos & men, he told me
i have his father's face

weird, he said
& i smiled like a sticker

i'm still trying too hard
to make my body a symbol

for the way love (re)shapes
itself into the world

moves room to room
watches youtube videos

on braiding hair, closet renovations
sleeping better

through dream, nistes & i write
thousands of poems

we drive on back roads
just for the fun of it

steering wheel cranked
forever turning

time in the body
is not

how i once imagined—
batteries in a jar

the blood of stars
pushed

from under our nails
time is tangled

up late into the early night
i unhook

orange beaded earrings
& the hours

it took to get here
place them beside my bed

like a glass of water
for morning

*

i accept the gift
of two coats from nohtâwiy

poke my arms into a puff
of feathers at sears

i learn in nêhiyawêwin
how to move verbs

kiwâpamin
you see me

kiwâpaminân
you see us

kiwâpaminâwâw
all of you I see

do you see the little slivers
of us circling water

the spot on my jacket
where feathers slip out & spill

back into the world
the work of (re)memory

is not a bubble or jump
through time

it is a thoughtful kiss
that leaves

any pain in the room
confessed, ruined

with touch
i'm tired of fear

what i'm trying to say
is english is failing me

the way memory
leaks

in december, nohtâwiy
takes me to the local pool hall

like a movie, so dim in there
when the door opens it creates

a momentary splash of sun
that makes my stomach lurch

though i can't explain why
i walk past

a vending machine with tootsie rolls
& sour keys near the bar

he teaches me how to angle
the cue, how to think in shadows

that's how you win
he says

the guys there, he knows them all by name
introduces me as daughter

shyly, & i turn into a mood ring
amber-violet-blue girl in the hall

*

i once shoved my foot through glass
getting to know my own anger

its patches of stupid
bloody love

stress is just a socially acceptable
word for fear

i'm ashamed of feeling too much

river edges like a cut
of laughter

left too long in the sun, a bloated
syringe of time between our kneecaps

i know you want
the piece of the story

that is clandestine
but i won't give it to you

& i'm not sorry
undo word after word

that tumbles out a sidewalk
undo textbooks

the science that renders
us invisible

undo your own heart, pull each vein
like unthreading a needle

hope is half-sung nêhiyawêwin
in a packed classroom

beading my cousin
a bolo in lime green

remember, love, we can
draw from all directions

of time, we can hover & gut
ourselves into new stories

be sad & not sad
about it all

ongoing conversations with nitêh

> listen for the hesitant beat
> sit at the edge of the woods
> shape shift around the defence
> ban the word *should*
> —Leanne Betasamosake Simpson

u are enough when a shower and a grey's anatomy episode
radically alters your day

when u become aster   beating lilac-yellow
antlered with hope

that first night on citalopram   u clap so hard
inside me   an applause of blades sharpens

my dreams   moonstruck and nervous
i'm awake even when i'm sleeping

i scotch-tape u to the sky
watch u pulse like an intersection above

directing each decision i've made back at me
i didn't move for a man i loved

i'm still waiting for nohtâwiy
in a crowded apartment

u are enough when scrambling eggs
when checking the mail in sweatpants is all u can do for today

ur tributaries bend
toward the ppl u love

branches of u held by them
carried through muscle memory

it's what we do in the after-space of regret that matters
now   u flood through this life into another

the tv version of urself bloody and exposed on the table
a bomb tucked against ur right atrium   drama's apex

meredith's hand touching mitêh
of what we've been afraid of lately

the bright-red possibility
we can destroy ourselves from the inside out

even if we've eaten our eggs   even if we care
it's ok to wonder   are we going to be *ok*?

the miraculous thing is u can stay alive outside of me
u can move body to body time through time   and survive

notes

The poem "meet cree: a practical guide to language" borrows its title from the book *Meet Cree: A Practical Guide to the Cree Language* by H. Christoph Wolfart and Janet F. Carroll (University of Alberta Press, 1973).

In "a run, a burn, a beck" the line "rock paper river" comes from the name of Faye HeavySheild's 2005 art exhibition at Gallery Connexion in Fredericton, New Brunswick.

"in six, the seasons" is indebted to the Gift of Language and Culture Project, an online language-learning resource.

The description of time as "tangled" in "all you can is the best you can" was borrowed from the poet Chris Abani, who described time as an entanglement on episode 61 of VS Podcast.

The phrase "star guts" in "minimal pairs are words holding hands" was inspired by a similar image from Danez Smith's poem "A note on vaseline."

"inside this hour / another hour inside / another hour" references the song "Lord, I Hope This Day Is Good" by Don Williams.

Humbled and grateful to Nadia Tepleski who shared with me the phrase, grief "is never not missing someone, it is living and missing at the same time," that appears in "with love."

The nêhiyawêwin questions and answers in "2.1.a   questions and answers" come directly from the section "2.1.a. questions and answers" in *mâci-nêhiyawêwin (Beginning Cree)* by Solomon Ratt (University of Regina Press, 2016).

Indebted to the brilliant mind of Brandi Bird who gifted me the line "i watch you say grace when my eyes should be closed" that appears in "emails with nohtâwiy."

Immense gratitude to the artwork of Joi T. Arcand, which inspired the poem "ᐸᐣᐴᐁᐤ" alongside early ideas about this collection. The poem "ᐸᐣᐴᐁᐤ" references two art pieces by Joi T. Arcand from the series "Wayfinding, 2017." The pieces referenced are ᑭᐣᐨ and ᐁᑲᐃᐧᐣ ᑐᐁᐃᐧᒉ. The final lines of the poem *"don't you dare be ashamed, don't you dare be shy"* are my translation of the piece ᐁᑲᐃᐧᐣ ᑐᐁᐃᐧᒉ.

acknowledgements

i am grateful and humbled to have crafted these poems on the traditional, ancestral and unceded territories of the Musqueam, Squamish and Tsleil-Waututh First Nations as well as the traditional, ancestral and unceded territories of the Cowichan Tribes.

many thanks to the following publications and their teams for publishing earlier versions of poems that appear in this collection: *Together Apart, The Fiddlehead, Room, Red Rising Magazine, SAD Mag, CV2, The New Quarterly*.

a version of "in six, the seasons" was shortlisted for the CBC Poetry Prize in 2016. versions of "conversations with nîton" and "have you ever fallen in love with a day?" were shortlisted for the CBC Poetry Prize in 2020.

a version of "minimal pairs are words holding hands" won *Room*'s poetry contest in 2018. many thanks to the organizers and the judge, Vivek Shraya. the poem was also selected for *Best Canadian Poetry in English 2020*. profound thanks to Marilyn Dumont for that honour.

a version of "a run, a burn, a beck". was selected for *Best Canadian Poetry in English 2018*. gratitude to Hoa Nguyen for including me.

versions of "in cree there is no word for half/brother" and "meet cree: a practical guide to language" won the National Magazine Award for Poetry in 2017.

profound thanks to the Nightwood Editions team, especially Emma and Silas, for their unwavering support and patience during the process of making this book. you gave my work a safe home and i am forever grateful. thank you to Angela for bringing this book to life with such a thoughtful and vibrant cover.

kinanâskomitin to the elders Darlene Willier, Dorothy Visser and Pauline Johnson for their nêhiyawêwin teachings, laughter and guidance. my reverence and gratitude runs deep.

kinanâskomitin to the many brilliant teachers whose feedback and support made this book possible: Rhea Tregebov (for always looking out for me), Ian Williams, Karen Solie, Sheryda Warrener, Eduardo C. Corral, Aisha Sasha John and Sandra Ridley.

kinanâskomitin to those whose work provided guidance, inspiration and awe: Jordan Abel, Liz Howard, Joshua Whitehead, Louise Bernice Halfe, Jessica Johns, Billy-Ray Belcourt, Brandi Bird, Emily Riddle, jaye simpson, Tommy Pico, Marilyn Dumont, Leanne Betasamosake Simpson, Katherena Vermette, Dallas Hunt, Layli Long Soldier and so many more.

kinanâskomitin to the incredible community of writers and artists i am lucky enough to be surrounded by. simply listing your names does not do justice to the amount of gratitude, care and love i have for you: Rachel (my brain twin), Jess, Jocelyn, Mica, Adrienne, Ellie, Mallory, Curtis, Brandi, Molly, Adèle, Dom, Kate, Shaun, Megan, Carter, Chris, Kyle, jaye, Emily, Justin, Evan, Oubah, Zoe, Kai, Annick, Sam, Savannah and so many more.

to Shaun: thank you for sharing your brilliant editorial eye. you gave this book a shape and i am so lucky to have had your poetic perspective.

to Molly: so grateful to have gone through this book journey with you.

immense gratitude for the late-night texts and manuscript phone calls. your editorial generosity helped make this book what it is.

to Brandi: my poetry twin and chosen family. thank you for everything. deep reverence, love and gratitude for your generous edits, encouragement and poetic brilliance—this book wouldn't be what it is without you.

kinanâskomitin to Eduardo C. Corral, Billy-Ray Belcourt and Liz Howard for your work, kind words and generosity.

to Jess: kinanâskomitin for your generous words and kinship.

kinanâskomitin to my pals in ottawa: Mike, Katie, Yosh, Dylan, Kalenga, Willow, Evie and so many more. you gifted me with a home away from home. immense gratitude for your friendships.

to my past loves. much of this book was written during my time with you. thank you for your support, encouragement and care.

kinanâskomitin to friends, roommates and chosen family: Julia, Nadia, Jenny, Cassie, Sonia, Larissa, Adam, Meg, Sadie, Jess, Janet and so many more. my love for you all is immense.

to J: thank you for being there during the final stages of writing this book. your love and care got me through.

kinanâskomitin to my family. with immense love and care for the parents i grew up with: Margaret and George. to all my aunties and uncles and cousins (especially Kyla and Catanne). to my grandparents. to nistes, my nieces and nephew. i cannot hold the amount of love i have for you all. nohkom—i carry you with me, always.

to nohtâwiy: this book is for you. forever sending my love and care.

finally, kinanâskomitin to you, dear reader. thank you for spending time with these poems.

about the author

Selina Boan is a white settler–nehiyaw poet living on the traditional, ancestral and unceded territories of the xʷməθkʷəy̓əm (Musqueam), səl̓ílwətaʔɬ (Tsleil-Waututh) and sḵwx̱wú7mesh (Squamish) First Nations. Her work has been published widely, including in *The Best Canadian Poetry 2018* and *2020*. She has received several honours for her work, including *Room*'s 2018 Emerging Writer Award and the 2017 National Magazine Award for Poetry. She is currently a poetry editor for Rahila's Ghost Press and is a member of the Growing Room Collective.

PHOTO CREDIT: KAYLA MACINNIS